Smart Money Moves A Guide for Teens and Elders to Financial Success

Willie Pedro

Copyright © [2023]

Title: Theni's Water: Potential, Quality, Perception, Health
Author's: Willie Pedro

This book was printed and published by [Publisher's: **Willie Pedro**] in [2023]

ISBN:

TABLE OF CONTENT

Chapter 10: Building a Lifetime of Financial Success 78

Chapter 1: The Basics of Money Management

Understanding the Importance of Financial Literacy

In today's complex and ever-changing financial landscape, it is becoming increasingly crucial for individuals of all ages to possess a strong foundation in financial literacy. Whether you are a teenager just starting to navigate the world of personal finance or an elder looking to make the most of your retirement savings, understanding the importance of financial literacy is paramount to achieving long-term financial success.

Financial literacy refers to the knowledge and skills necessary to make informed and effective decisions about money. It encompasses a wide range of topics, including budgeting, saving, investing, credit management, and understanding financial products and services. By becoming financially literate, individuals gain the tools and knowledge needed to make sound financial choices, avoid common pitfalls, and ultimately achieve their financial goals.

For teenagers, developing financial literacy skills early on can set them up for a lifetime of financial success. Learning how to create and stick to a budget, save for future goals, and distinguish between needs and wants are all essential money management tips that can help teens make smart financial decisions as they grow older. Moreover, understanding the importance of credit scores, interest rates, and how to manage debt can help teens avoid financial hardships in the future.

For elders, financial literacy is equally vital. Retirement planning, managing investments, and understanding complex financial products can be overwhelming for those who haven't had prior exposure to these concepts. By equipping themselves with financial literacy skills, elders can confidently navigate their retirement years, ensuring their hard-earned savings are maximized and protected. Additionally, being financially literate empowers elders to make informed decisions about estate planning, long-term care, and other important financial considerations.

Regardless of age, financial literacy is a lifelong journey. The world of personal finance is constantly evolving, and staying informed about new trends, regulations, and opportunities is key to maintaining financial stability. By regularly seeking out resources, attending workshops, and engaging in ongoing financial education, individuals can continuously enhance their financial literacy and adapt to the ever-changing financial landscape.

In conclusion, understanding the importance of financial literacy is essential for individuals of all ages, whether they are teenagers just starting their financial journey or elders seeking to make the most of their retirement savings. By developing strong financial literacy skills, individuals can make informed decisions, avoid financial pitfalls, and ultimately achieve their long-term financial goals.

Setting Financial Goals

Setting financial goals is an essential step towards achieving financial success, regardless of your age. Whether you are a teenager just starting to earn money or an elder looking to improve your financial situation, having clear goals can help you stay focused, motivated, and make smart money moves. In this subchapter, we will explore the importance of setting financial goals and provide practical tips to help you get started.

Why set financial goals? The answer is simple. Without goals, it is easy to lose track of your financial progress and make impulsive decisions that may hinder your financial well-being. By setting goals, you establish a roadmap that guides your financial decisions and helps you prioritize your spending and saving habits.

For teens, financial goals could include saving for college tuition, buying a car, or starting a small business. Elders, on the other hand, may have goals such as paying off mortgage debt, building a retirement fund, or leaving a financial legacy for their children. Regardless of your age, it is crucial to set realistic and achievable goals that align with your financial situation and long-term aspirations.

To set financial goals effectively, start by assessing your current financial status. Evaluate your income, expenses, and debt, if any. This will give you a clear picture of where you stand financially and help you identify areas that require improvement. Next, prioritize your goals based on their importance and urgency. It is essential to set both short-term and long-term goals to ensure a balanced approach.

Once you have defined your goals, break them down into smaller, manageable steps. For instance, if your goal is to save $10,000 for a down payment on a house, set monthly or weekly saving targets to track your progress. Consider automating your savings by setting up automatic transfers from your paycheck or checking account to a separate savings account to make the process easier.

Regularly review and revise your goals as your financial circumstances change. Life is unpredictable, and your goals may need adjustment along the way. Stay flexible and adapt your plans accordingly.

In conclusion, setting financial goals is a crucial step towards financial success for both teens and elders. By establishing clear goals, you gain clarity, motivation, and direction in managing your money effectively. Remember to assess your current financial situation, prioritize your goals, break them down into smaller steps, and regularly review and revise them as needed. With proper goal-setting, you can make smart money moves and achieve your financial dreams.

Creating a Budget

Managing your finances is an essential life skill that everyone should learn, regardless of age. Whether you are a teenager navigating your first part-time job or an elder looking to make the most of your retirement savings, creating a budget is a fundamental step towards financial success. In this subchapter, we will explore the importance of budgeting and provide practical tips on how to create an effective budget that works for you.

A budget is simply a plan that helps you track your income and expenses. It serves as a roadmap for your financial journey, enabling you to allocate your resources wisely and prioritize your financial goals. By creating a budget, you gain control over your money, reduce financial stress, and pave the way for financial security and success.

For teens, budgeting can be particularly beneficial as it instills good money management habits early on. It teaches you the value of saving, setting financial goals, and making informed spending decisions. Start by listing your income sources, such as allowance, part-time job earnings, or monetary gifts. Next, track your expenses, categorizing them into essentials (like food and transportation) and non-essentials such as entertainment and shopping). This exercise will help you identify areas where you can cut back and save.

As an elder, budgeting becomes even more crucial, especially when living on a fixed income. Begin by determining your monthly income from sources like pensions, social security, or investments. List all your expenses, including housing, healthcare, insurance, and daily living costs. It is essential to factor in emergency funds and allocate some money towards savings or investments. Prioritize your expenses, ensuring that you cover your essential needs first and then allocate funds for discretionary spending.

Remember, creating a budget is not a one-time activity. You should review and adjust it periodically to accommodate any changes in your income, expenses, or financial goals. It may take some time and effort to find a budgeting system that suits you best, whether it's using an app, spreadsheet, or a traditional pen and paper method. The key is to be consistent, disciplined, and flexible in your approach.

In conclusion, regardless of your age, creating a budget is a vital step towards financial success. It empowers you to take control of your money, make informed decisions, and achieve your financial goals. So, start budgeting today and pave the way for a brighter financial future.

Chapter 2: Saving and Investing

The Power of Saving

In this subchapter, we will delve into the remarkable power of saving and how it can transform your financial future. Whether you are a teenager just starting your journey into money management or an elder looking to secure your retirement, the concept of saving is universal and timeless.

Saving money is not only about setting funds aside for emergencies or big-ticket purchases; it is a powerful tool that can help you build wealth, achieve financial independence, and enjoy a stress-free life. Let's explore the various ways saving can benefit both teens and elders.

For teenagers, saving money is an essential habit to cultivate early on. It teaches financial discipline, patience, and delayed gratification. By setting aside a portion of their income, teens can create a safety net for unexpected expenses and develop a sense of financial responsibility. Saving can also empower young people to achieve their goals, whether it's saving for college, starting a business, or traveling the world.

For elders, saving money becomes even more crucial. It provides a sense of security during retirement, ensuring a comfortable lifestyle and peace of mind. By saving consistently and taking advantage of investment opportunities, elders can grow their nest egg and maintain their financial independence. Saving also allows them to leave a legacy for their loved ones, ensuring financial stability for future generations.

Regardless of age, the power of saving lies in its compounding effect. By consistently saving a portion of your income, you can harness the power of compound interest, where your money grows over time. This means that even small contributions can have a significant impact on your savings, as they generate interest and accumulate over the years.

To make the most of your saving potential, it is vital to develop good money management habits. Create a budget that outlines your income, expenses, and savings goals. Automate your savings by setting up automatic transfers from your paycheck to a dedicated savings account. Take advantage of tax-advantaged retirement accounts, such as 401(k)s or IRAs, to maximize your savings and potential tax benefits.

In conclusion, the power of saving cannot be overstated. Whether you are a teenager or an elder, saving money is a fundamental step towards financial success. It provides financial stability, security, and the ability to achieve your dreams. By embracing the power of saving, you are setting yourself on the path to a brighter and more prosperous future.

Different Types of Savings Accounts

When it comes to saving money, it's important to choose the right savings account that suits your needs. There are various types of savings accounts available, each designed to cater to different financial goals and circumstances. In this subchapter, we will explore the different types of savings accounts and how they can benefit both teens and elders in their quest for financial success.

1. Basic Savings Account: This is the most common type of savings account offered by banks and credit unions. It provides a safe place to store your money while earning a small amount of interest. Basic savings accounts are a great option for beginners or those who want easy access to their funds.

2. High-Yield Savings Account: For those looking to maximize their savings, a high-yield savings account is a great choice. These accounts offer higher interest rates than basic savings accounts, allowing your money to grow at a faster pace. High-yield savings accounts are ideal for teens or elders who have surplus funds and want to earn more from their savings.

3. Money Market Account: Money market accounts are similar to savings accounts but typically offer higher interest rates. They require a higher minimum balance and may have limited check-writing capabilities. Money market accounts are a good option for those who want to earn a higher return on their savings without taking on too much risk.

4. Certificate of Deposit (CD): A CD is a fixed-term savings account that offers a higher interest rate in exchange for locking your money away for a specific period, ranging from months to years. CDs are an

excellent choice for teens or elders who have long-term savings goals and don't need immediate access to their funds.

5. Individual Retirement Account (IRA): An IRA is a retirement savings account that offers tax advantages. There are two main types of IRAs: traditional and Roth. Traditional IRAs allow you to contribute pre-tax dollars, while Roth IRAs allow for tax-free withdrawals in retirement. IRAs are beneficial for both teens and elders who want to save for retirement and enjoy tax advantages.

Choosing the right savings account is crucial for achieving financial success. By understanding the different types of savings accounts available, teens and elders can make informed decisions that align with their financial goals. Whether it's a basic savings account for easy access to funds or a high-yield savings account for accelerated growth, there is a savings account option for everyone. So, take the first step towards financial success by selecting the savings account that best suits your needs and start saving today!

Introduction to Investing

Investing is an essential aspect of financial planning and building wealth. Whether you are a teenager just starting to earn money or an elder looking to secure your retirement, understanding the fundamentals of investing is crucial. In this subchapter, we will introduce you to the world of investing and equip you with the knowledge and tools necessary to make informed investment decisions.

Investing is essentially the act of putting your money to work to generate returns over time. Instead of merely saving money in a bank account, investing allows you to grow your wealth by taking advantage of various investment vehicles such as stocks, bonds, mutual funds, real estate, and more.

For teenagers, investing at a young age can set them on the path to financial success. By starting early, they can benefit from the power of compounding, allowing their investments to grow exponentially over time. Elders, on the other hand, may have different investment goals, such as generating passive income or preserving capital for retirement.

Before diving into the world of investing, it is crucial to have a solid understanding of your financial goals and risk tolerance. Identifying your objectives will help you determine the appropriate investment strategies and asset allocation that align with your needs.

In this subchapter, we will cover the basics of different investment options, including stocks, bonds, and mutual funds. We will explain key investment concepts such as risk and return, diversification, and asset allocation. Additionally, we will discuss the importance of conducting thorough research and due diligence before making any investment decisions.

Furthermore, we will provide valuable tips and insights on how to navigate the investment landscape successfully. We will discuss the importance of setting realistic expectations, staying disciplined, and avoiding common investment pitfalls.

By the end of this subchapter, you will have a solid foundation in investing, allowing you to make informed decisions that align with your financial goals and risk tolerance. Whether you are a teenager or an elder, investing can play a significant role in securing your financial future. So, let's dive into the world of investing and embark on a journey towards financial success!

Building a Diversified Portfolio

When it comes to managing your finances and ensuring long-term financial success, building a diversified portfolio is a crucial step. This subchapter will provide valuable insights and tips on how to create a well-rounded investment strategy that can benefit both teens and elders.

Diversification is the practice of spreading your investments across various asset classes, such as stocks, bonds, real estate, and mutual funds, among others. The idea behind this strategy is to reduce risk by not putting all your eggs in one basket. By diversifying your portfolio, you can potentially minimize the impact of market volatility and increase the likelihood of achieving consistent returns over time.

For teens who are just starting their financial journey, building a diversified portfolio can set them up for long-term success. It's important to start early, taking advantage of the power of compounding. By investing in a mix of high-risk and low-risk assets, teens can begin to grow their wealth and learn valuable lessons about the market.

Elders, on the other hand, can also benefit from diversification. As retirement approaches, it's essential to protect the wealth accumulated over the years and ensure a steady income stream. By diversifying their investments, elders can safeguard against potential market downturns and protect their retirement savings.

So, how can you build a diversified portfolio? First, assess your financial goals, risk tolerance, and time horizon. This will help determine the appropriate asset allocation for your portfolio. Next, research and select a mix of investments that align with your goals.

Consider diversifying across different geographic regions, industries, and sectors.

Additionally, consider investing in index funds or exchange-traded funds (ETFs), which provide instant diversification by tracking broad market indexes. These funds are typically low-cost and provide exposure to a wide range of assets.

Remember, building a diversified portfolio is an ongoing process. Regularly review and rebalance your portfolio to ensure it remains aligned with your goals and risk tolerance. As you gain more experience and knowledge, you can make adjustments and fine-tune your investment strategy.

In conclusion, building a diversified portfolio is essential for both teens and elders seeking financial success. By spreading your investments across different asset classes, you can reduce risk and increase the potential for consistent returns over time. Start early assess your goals and risk tolerance, and regularly review and rebalance your portfolio. With a diversified portfolio, you can navigate the ever-changing financial landscape and achieve long-term financial security.

Chapter 3: Earning and Managing Income

Exploring Different Job Opportunities

When it comes to financial success, exploring different job opportunities is an essential step for both teens and elders. Whether you are a young individual looking to start your career or an elder seeking additional income or fulfillment, understanding the various job options available can help you make smarter money moves.

For teenagers, getting a part-time job during high school or college can be a great way to earn money while learning valuable skills. Some popular job opportunities for teens include working at local stores, restaurants, or even babysitting. These jobs not only provide a steady income but also teach important lessons about responsibility, time management, and customer service. Additionally, part-time jobs can help teenagers develop a strong work ethic and become financially independent at an early age.

Elders, on the other hand, may be looking for job opportunities to supplement their retirement income or to explore new interests and stay engaged. Many seniors find joy in part-time work such as tutoring, consulting, or working as a greeter at a local store. These jobs not only provide financial stability but also offer opportunities for social interaction and personal growth. Additionally, some organizations offer programs specifically designed for seniors, allowing them to utilize their years of experience and expertise.

Furthermore, the advent of the internet has opened up a plethora of job opportunities for people of all ages. Online freelancing platforms, such as Upwork or Fiverr, allow individuals to offer their skills and services remotely. This is particularly beneficial for teenagers and elders, as it provides flexibility and the ability to work from home. Whether it's graphic design, writing, or virtual assistance, there are countless online job opportunities available to explore.

When exploring different job opportunities, it's important to consider your skills, interests, and long-term goals. Finding a job that aligns with your passions and strengths can lead to greater job satisfaction and financial success. Additionally, networking and seeking advice from professionals in your desired field can provide valuable insights and open doors to exciting opportunities.

In conclusion, exploring different job opportunities is crucial for both teens and elders on their journey towards financial success. Whether it's part-time jobs, freelancing, or even starting your own business, the world is full of possibilities. By being proactive, staying open-minded, and leveraging your unique skills and experiences, you can find fulfilling job opportunities that not only provide financial stability but also contribute to personal growth and happiness.

Developing Marketable Skills

In today's rapidly changing and highly competitive job market, it is essential to possess marketable skills that can set you apart from the crowd. Whether you are a teenager just starting to think about your future or an elder looking to enhance your financial prospects, developing these skills is crucial for financial success. This subchapter will outline practical strategies for individuals of all ages to cultivate marketable skills and unlock new opportunities.

1. Identify Your Strengths: Begin by identifying your strengths and interests. What are you passionate about? What skills do you excel in? Understanding your strengths will help you focus on areas where you can naturally excel, increasing your chances of success.

2. Research In-Demand Skills: Stay updated on the rapidly evolving job market by researching in-demand skills. Technology-related skills, such as coding, data analysis, and digital marketing, are highly sought after. Additionally, soft skills like communication, leadership, and problem-solving are universally valuable and can be honed.

3. Pursue Education and Training: Invest in your education and seek out training programs to develop your marketable skills. Consider enrolling in online courses, attending workshops, or pursuing a degree in your field of interest. Many resources are available, often at low cost or even for free, making continuous learning accessible to everyone.

4. Gain Practical Experience: While education is essential, practical experience is equally valuable. Seek internships, apprenticeships, or volunteer opportunities to gain hands-on experience in your chosen field. Practical experience not only enhances your skills but also

demonstrates your commitment and dedication to potential employers.

5. Network and Build Relationships: Networking plays a significant role in developing marketable skills. Attend industry events, join professional associations, and connect with individuals in your desired field. Networking can lead to mentorship opportunities, job referrals, and invaluable insights into the job market.

6. Embrace Lifelong Learning: Keep an open mind and embrace lifelong learning. The job market is ever-evolving, and new skills are constantly emerging. By staying curious and continuously adapting, you can remain relevant and increase your marketability.

7. Showcase Your Skills: Finally, effectively showcase your skills to potential employers or clients. Create a professional resume, build an online portfolio, and leverage social media platforms to highlight your achievements and capabilities. Additionally, consider obtaining certifications or licenses that validate your skills and enhance your credibility.

In conclusion, developing marketable skills is crucial for both teens and elders seeking financial success. By identifying your strengths, researching in-demand skills, pursuing education and training, gaining practical experience, networking, embracing lifelong learning, and showcasing your skills, you can position yourself for success in today's competitive job market. Remember, investing in your skills is an investment in your future.

Understanding Taxes and Deductions

Taxes and deductions can be complex and intimidating for individuals of all ages, but it is crucial to have a good grasp of these concepts in order to achieve financial success. Whether you are a teenager just starting to earn your own money or an elder looking to manage your finances wisely, this subchapter will provide you with valuable insights on taxes and deductions.

Taxes are the way governments collect money to fund public services and infrastructure. They are levied on various types of income, including wages, salaries, and investment profits. Understanding how taxes work is essential to effectively managing your finances. In this subchapter, we will explore different types of taxes, such as income tax, property tax, and sales tax, and discuss how they impact your financial situation.

Additionally, we will delve into the world of deductions. Deductions are expenses that can be subtracted from your taxable income, reducing the amount of tax you owe. It is crucial to identify which deductions you qualify for, as they can significantly lower your tax liability. Common deductions include medical expenses, charitable donations, and mortgage interest payments. By understanding the deductions available to you, you can maximize your tax savings and keep more money in your pocket.

For teenagers, learning about taxes and deductions early on can set them up for financial success in the future. By understanding the importance of paying taxes and how deductions can reduce their tax burden, teens can develop responsible money management habits that will serve them well throughout their lives.

Elders, on the other hand, may face different tax considerations. They may be eligible for additional deductions, such as those related to retirement savings or healthcare expenses. Understanding these deductions can help elders make informed financial decisions and ensure they are taking full advantage of the benefits available to them.

In this subchapter, we will provide practical tips and strategies to help both teens and elders navigate the complex world of taxes and deductions. By demystifying these concepts and providing clear explanations, we aim to empower our readers to make smart money moves and achieve financial success.

Remember, taxes and deductions are not something to fear but rather an opportunity to optimize your finances. With the knowledge gained from this subchapter, you will be well-equipped to make informed decisions that will have a positive impact on your financial well-being.

Effective Strategies for Managing Income

Managing income effectively is essential for individuals of all ages. Whether you are a teenager just starting to earn money or an elder looking to make the most of your retirement income, implementing effective strategies can help you achieve financial success. This subchapter aims to provide valuable money management tips for teens and elders, offering practical advice that can be applied to various financial situations.

1. Budgeting: Creating a budget is the foundation of effective income management. Start by tracking your expenses and income, then allocate your money wisely. Prioritize essential expenses such as housing, utilities, and food, and set aside a portion for savings or investments.

2. Saving and Investing: Regardless of your age, saving and investing should be a priority. Learn about different saving and investment options that suit your financial goals and risk tolerance. Consider opening a savings account, investing in stocks or mutual funds, or exploring retirement accounts like an IRA or 401(k).

3. Minimizing Debt: Debt can hinder your financial progress. Minimize unnecessary debts by practicing responsible borrowing and avoiding excessive use of credit cards. Prioritize paying off high-interest debts first, and seek professional advice if you find yourself overwhelmed by debt.

4. Multiple Income Streams: Instead of relying solely on a single source of income, explore opportunities to diversify your earnings. Teens can consider part-time jobs or entrepreneurial ventures, while elders can explore hobbies or consulting services. Multiple income streams can provide financial stability and enhance your overall income management.

5. Insurance: Protecting your assets and income is crucial for financial security. Consider purchasing appropriate insurance coverage to safeguard against unexpected events. This includes health insurance, life insurance, disability insurance, and homeowner's or renter's insurance.

6. Regular Financial Check-Ups: Make it a habit to review your financial situation regularly. Assess your budget, track your expenses, and evaluate your progress towards your financial goals. Adjust your strategies as needed to ensure you stay on track.

7. Seek Professional Advice: If you feel overwhelmed or unsure about managing your income effectively, don't hesitate to seek professional

advice. Consult financial advisors, accountants, or mentors who can provide expert guidance tailored to your specific circumstances.

By implementing these effective strategies for managing income, individuals of all ages can improve their financial well-being. Whether you are a teenager looking to establish good money habits or an elder seeking financial security in retirement, these tips will help you make smart money moves and achieve long-term financial success.

Chapter 4: Credit and Debt Management

Building Good Credit

In today's society, having good credit is essential for financial success. Whether you are a teenager just entering the world of personal finance or an elder looking to improve your financial standing, building good credit should be a top priority. This subchapter will provide you with valuable insights and practical tips on how to establish and maintain a strong credit history.

Understanding the Importance of Credit

Before delving into the specifics of building good credit, it's crucial to understand why credit matters. Your credit history is a record of your financial responsibility, and it plays a significant role in your ability to secure loans, rent apartments, and even land a job. Lenders, landlords, and employers use your credit score as an indicator of your trustworthiness and reliability.

Establishing Credit as a Teen

If you are a teenager, now is the perfect time to start building your credit. Begin by opening a checking and savings account in your name, as this demonstrates financial responsibility. Consider applying for a secured credit card, which requires a cash deposit as collateral. Make small purchases with your card and always pay off the balance in full each month to establish a positive payment history.

Building Good Credit as an Elder

As an elder, you may already have an established credit history. However, it's essential to maintain and improve it. Start by reviewing your credit report regularly to ensure its accuracy and dispute any errors you find. Pay all your bills on time, as late payments can significantly impact your credit score. Additionally, keep your credit card balances low and avoid opening multiple new accounts simultaneously.

Tips for Everyone

Regardless of your age, certain strategies can help you build and maintain good credit. Firstly, avoid excessive borrowing. Only take out loans or use credit for essential purchases that you can comfortably afford to repay. Secondly, be mindful of your credit utilization ratio, which is the amount of credit you use compared to your total available credit. Aim to keep this ratio below 30% to demonstrate responsible credit management.

Lastly, be patient. Building good credit takes time, and it's not achieved overnight. Stay committed to making smart financial choices, and your credit score will gradually improve.

In conclusion, building good credit is a critical step towards financial success, whether you are a teenager or an elder. By understanding the importance of credit, establishing credit early, and following responsible financial habits, you can ensure a strong credit history that will open doors to various opportunities throughout your life.

Responsible Borrowing

In today's world, where credit cards and loans are readily available, it is crucial to understand the concept of responsible borrowing. Whether you are a teenager just starting to handle money or an elder looking to manage your finances wisely, this subchapter will provide you with valuable insights and tips on how to borrow money responsibly.

Borrowing money can be tempting, especially when faced with unexpected expenses or desires for the latest gadgets or fashion trends. However, it is essential to remember that borrowed money is not free money; it comes with interest and repayment terms that can impact your financial future.

The first step towards responsible borrowing is to assess your needs versus wants. Before taking on any debt, ask yourself whether it is a necessary expense or merely a desire. By prioritizing your needs and cutting down on unnecessary spending, you can reduce the need for borrowing in the first place.

If borrowing becomes necessary, it is crucial to research and compare different borrowing options. Evaluate the interest rates, repayment terms, and any additional fees associated with each option. This will help you choose the most suitable option that aligns with your financial goals and capabilities.

Furthermore, it is vital to borrow only what you can afford to repay comfortably. Before taking on any debt, assess your income, expenses, and existing financial obligations. Create a realistic budget that allows you to allocate a portion of your income towards debt repayment without compromising your essential needs.

Responsible borrowing also involves maintaining a good credit history. Your credit score plays a significant role in determining your eligibility for loans and the interest rates you are offered. To build and maintain a good credit score, it is crucial to make timely repayments, avoid maxing out credit cards, and keep your credit utilization ratio low.

Lastly, it is important to have a plan for repaying borrowed money. Create a repayment schedule and stick to it. Paying off your debts as soon as possible will not only save you money on interest but also improve your financial well-being in the long run.

In conclusion, responsible borrowing is a vital aspect of money management for both teens and elders. By prioritizing needs, researching borrowing options, borrowing within your means, maintaining good credit, and having a repayment plan, you can make smart borrowing decisions that contribute to your financial success. Remember, borrowing should be a tool to improve your life, not a burden that weighs you down.

Understanding Credit Scores

One crucial aspect of managing your finances effectively is understanding credit scores. Whether you are a teenager just beginning to navigate the world of personal finance or an elder looking to make smart money moves, having a good grasp of credit scores is essential. In this subchapter, we will delve into the basics of credit scores, their significance, and how you can improve yours.

A credit score is a three-digit number that represents your creditworthiness to lenders. It is based on your credit history and is used by financial institutions to determine your eligibility for loans, credit cards, and other forms of credit. A higher credit score indicates a lower risk to lenders, making it easier for you to secure loans and credit at favorable interest rates.

To understand credit scores better, it is important to know the factors that influence them. Payment history, which includes your track record of making timely payments, carries the most significant weight, accounting for about 35% of your credit score. The amounts owed, length of credit history, types of credit used, and new credit applications also impact your score.

For teens, it is crucial to establish good credit habits early on. This includes making payments on time, not maxing out credit cards, and keeping credit utilization low. Elders, on the other hand, may need to focus on maintaining a good credit score or improving it if necessary. By understanding these factors and how they affect your credit score, you can take proactive steps to improve your financial standing.

Building and maintaining a good credit score is vital for various reasons. It not only enables you to access credit when needed but also opens doors to better financial opportunities, such as lower interest rates, higher credit limits, and favorable terms on loans. Additionally, a good credit score can positively impact other areas of your life, including insurance premiums, rental applications, and even job opportunities.

In the subsequent sections of this subchapter, we will explore practical tips and strategies to improve your credit score. From managing your debts effectively to disputing errors on your credit report, we will empower you with the knowledge and tools necessary to take control of your credit score and ultimately achieve financial success.

Remember, understanding credit scores is a vital component of money management for teens and elders alike. By mastering this aspect of personal finance, you can pave the way for a brighter financial future and make smart money moves that will benefit you throughout your life.

Strategies for Debt Repayment

Debt can be a burden that weighs heavily on individuals of all ages. Whether you are a teen making your first financial decisions or an elder looking to secure your financial future, implementing effective strategies for debt repayment is crucial. In this chapter, we will explore some smart money moves that can help you manage and eliminate debt.

1. Create a Budget: The first step towards debt repayment is understanding your current financial situation. Start by creating a budget that outlines your monthly income and expenses. Identify areas where you can cut back and allocate more funds towards debt repayment.

2. Prioritize Debts: Not all debts are created equal. Focus on paying off high-interest debts first, such as credit card balances or personal loans. Make minimum payments on lower-interest debts while putting extra money towards the high-interest ones. This strategy will help you save money on interest payments in the long run.

. Negotiate with Creditors: If you find yourself struggling to meet your debt obligations, don't hesitate to reach out to your creditors. Many creditors are willing to negotiate lower interest rates or create a more manageable repayment plan. Communication is key in finding a solution that works for both parties involved.

. Snowball Method: This debt repayment strategy involves paying off your smallest debts first while making minimum payments on larger debts. Once the smallest debt is paid off, take the money you were allocating towards it and add it to the minimum payment of the next smallest debt. This method builds momentum and motivates you to keep going.

5. Seek Professional Help: If your debts have become overwhelming, consider seeking professional help from a credit counseling agency or a reputable financial advisor. They can help you create a realistic debt repayment plan and provide guidance on managing your finances more effectively.

Remember, the journey to becoming debt-free requires patience, discipline, and consistency. Celebrate small victories along the way and stay committed to your financial goals. By implementing these strategies, you will be on your way to achieving financial success and enjoying the peace of mind that comes with being debt-free.

Whether you are a teen just starting your financial journey or an elder looking to secure your financial future, these strategies for debt repayment will empower you to take control of your finances and pave the way for a brighter financial future.

Chapter 5: Smart Spending Habits

Differentiating Needs vs. Wants

In today's consumer-driven society, it can be challenging to distinguish between our needs and wants. We are constantly bombarded with advertisements and peer pressure, enticing us to buy the latest gadgets, trendy clothes, and luxurious items. However, understanding the difference between needs and wants is crucial for effective money management. In this subchapter, we will explore the importance of differentiating between needs and wants, and how it can lead to financial success for both teens and elders.

First and foremost, let's define needs and wants. Needs are the essential things necessary for our survival and well-being, such as food, shelter, clothing, and healthcare. On the other hand, wants are the desires and non-essential items that we can live without, such as expensive vacations, designer clothes, or the latest smartphone.

Teens, who are often starting to earn their own money or receiving allowances, tend to be more susceptible to impulse buying and succumbing to peer pressure. Understanding the difference between needs and wants is crucial for them to develop healthy financial habits from an early age. By prioritizing needs over wants, teens can save money for more meaningful and important goals, like education or future investments. Learning to delay gratification can be a valuable lesson in achieving long-term financial success.

Elders, on the other hand, may face different challenges when it comes to distinguishing between needs and wants. Retirement often comes with a fixed income, and it becomes even more important to allocate resources wisely. By carefully evaluating their expenses and identifying true needs versus wants, elders can ensure a more secure and comfortable retirement. This includes things like downsizing to a smaller home, cutting back on unnecessary expenses, and prioritizing health and well-being.

To differentiate between needs and wants, it is essential to ask ourselves a few key questions. Is this item necessary for my survival and well-being? Can I live without it? Will it contribute to my long-term goals? Taking a moment to reflect on these questions can help us make sound financial decisions.

In conclusion, understanding the difference between needs and wants is a fundamental aspect of money management for both teens and elders. By prioritizing needs over wants, individuals can save money, achieve their financial goals, and lead a more fulfilled life. Developing this skill at an early age will set teens on a path to financial success while elders can make the most of their retirement years. Remember it's not about depriving ourselves of the things we want, but rather finding a balance that aligns with our financial goals and priorities.

Comparison Shopping and Negotiation Skills

In today's fast-paced and consumer-driven world, it's crucial for individuals of all ages to develop strong money management skills. Whether you're a teen starting to navigate the financial world or an elder looking to make the most of your hard-earned savings, understanding the importance of comparison shopping and negotiation skills can significantly impact your financial success.

Comparison shopping is the process of evaluating different products or services to find the best value for your money. By researching and comparing prices, features, and quality, you can make informed decisions that align with your budget and needs. This practice is especially vital for teens who may have limited income or elders who are living on a fixed budget.

One of the most accessible ways to compare prices is by utilizing online platforms and apps. These tools allow you to search for products or services and compare prices from various retailers or providers. Additionally, take advantage of customer reviews and ratings to gain insight into the quality and reliability of a particular item.

However, comparison shopping is not limited to online platforms. Visiting physical stores and talking to sales representatives can provide valuable information and even lead to better deals. Remember to inquire about warranties, return policies, and any additional costs associated with the product or service before making a final decision.

In addition to comparison shopping, negotiation skills can help you save money and attain better deals. This skill is essential for individuals of all ages, as it can be used in various situations, such as purchasing a car, negotiating rent, or even haggling at a flea market.

To become a proficient negotiator, start by doing thorough research on the item or service you wish to acquire. Understand the market value, competitors' prices, and any ongoing promotions or discounts. Armed with this knowledge, you can confidently negotiate for a better price or additional benefits.

Practice active listening and effective communication during negotiations. Be respectful, assertive, and willing to compromise. Remember that negotiation is a two-way street, and finding a win-win situation is the ultimate goal.

Developing comparison shopping and negotiation skills is an ongoing process. By continuously honing these abilities, you can save money, make wise financial decisions, and achieve your long-term financial goals. Whether you're a teen or an elder, embracing these skills will empower you to take control of your finances and pave the way for a financially successful future.

Managing Impulse Buying

Impulse buying is a common behavior that can have a negative impact on your financial well-being. Whether you are a teenager or an elder, learning how to manage impulse buying is an essential skill for achieving financial success. In this subchapter, we will explore some practical strategies that will help you curb your impulsive spending habits and make smarter money moves.

One of the first steps in managing impulse buying is understanding the root causes of this behavior. Impulse buying often stems from emotions such as boredom, stress, or a desire for instant gratification. By recognizing these triggers, you can develop alternative ways to cope with these emotions that don't involve spending money. Engaging in hobbies, practicing meditation, or seeking support from friends and family are just a few examples of healthier alternatives.

Creating a budget is another crucial tool in managing impulse buying. By setting limits on your spending and allocating specific amounts for different categories, you can gain control over your finances. Be sure to include a discretionary spending category in your budget, which allows for small indulgences without derailing your financial goals. Stick to your budget and resist the urge to make impulsive purchases that are not aligned with your priorities.

Another effective strategy for managing impulse buying is practicing delayed gratification. Before making a purchase, give yourself a cooling-off period of at least 24 hours. This will allow you to evaluate whether the item is a genuine need or just a fleeting desire. Often, you will find that the urge to buy dissipates over time, saving you from regretful purchases.

Utilizing technology can also help in managing impulse buying. Many financial apps and online tools offer features that track your spending, send alerts for exceeded budgets, and provide insights into your purchasing patterns. By leveraging these resources, you can gain a better understanding of your spending habits and identify areas where you tend to make impulsive purchases.

In conclusion, managing impulse buying is a crucial skill for both teens and elders to achieve financial success. By recognizing the triggers, creating a budget, practicing delayed gratification, and utilizing technology, you can take control of your impulsive spending habits and make smarter money moves. Remember, financial success is built on thoughtful and intentional decision-making, rather than impulsive actions.

Strategies for Saving on Everyday Expenses

In today's fast-paced world, managing our finances has become more important than ever. Whether you're a teenager just starting to learn about money or an elder looking to make the most of your retirement savings, finding ways to save on everyday expenses can make a significant difference in your financial success. This subchapter will provide you with practical strategies to help you stretch your dollars further and make smart money moves.

1. Create a budget: Start by tracking your income and expenses. This will give you a clear picture of where your money is going and where you can make adjustments. Allocate a certain amount of money for each category, such as groceries, transportation, and entertainment, and stick to it.

2. Cut back on unnecessary expenses: Identify areas where you can make cutbacks without sacrificing your quality of life. For example, consider brewing your own coffee instead of buying it daily or canceling subscriptions you rarely use.

. Compare prices: Before making a purchase, do your research and compare prices from different stores or online retailers. Take advantage of coupons, discounts, and sales to get the best deal.

. Buy in bulk: When it comes to non-perishable items or items you frequently use, buying in bulk can save you money in the long run. Must be mindful of expiration dates and storage space.

Cook at home: Eating out can quickly drain your budget. Learn to cook simple and nutritious meals at home. Involve your family or friends in meal planning and preparation to make it a fun and cost-effective activity.

6. Use public transportation or carpool: Reduce your transportation expenses by utilizing public transportation whenever possible. If you have colleagues or neighbors who live nearby, consider carpooling to share the cost of commuting.

7. Embrace energy-saving habits: Lower your utility bills by adopting energy-saving habits. Turn off lights and unplug electronics when not in use, use natural lighting whenever possible, and adjust your thermostat to save on heating and cooling costs.

8. Shop second-hand: Thrift stores, consignment shops, and online marketplaces offer great deals on clothing, furniture, and other items. Give them a chance before buying brand-new items.

By implementing these strategies, you will be well on your way to saving money on everyday expenses and achieving financial success. Remember, it's the small changes that add up over time and make a big difference. Start today and take control of your financial future.

Chapter 6: Financial Planning for the Future

Retirement Planning

Retirement is a phase of life that we all look forward to, but to ensure a secure and comfortable retirement, proper planning is essential. In this subchapter, we will delve into the intricacies of retirement planning, providing valuable insights and actionable steps for both teens and elders to achieve financial success in their golden years.

For teens, it's never too early to start thinking about retirement. The power of compound interest can work wonders if you begin saving early. We will discuss the importance of setting financial goals, creating a budget, and developing a savings plan. Additionally, we will explore various investment options that can help teens grow their money over time, such as individual retirement accounts (IRAs) or 401(k) plans. By establishing good money habits at a young age, teens can set themselves up for a secure retirement and financial independence.

For elders, retirement planning may involve different considerations. We will discuss strategies to maximize Social Security benefits, manage healthcare costs, and make smart investment decisions during retirement. We will emphasize the importance of having a diversified investment portfolio and adjusting it as one approaches retirement to mitigate risk. Moreover, we will explore options for generating passive income, such as rental properties or dividend-paying stocks, to ensure steady cash flow during retirement.

Regardless of age, we will also address the significance of having an emergency fund to cover unexpected expenses and potential health issues. We will provide guidance on how to calculate retirement needs based on estimated expenses and the desired lifestyle. Additionally, we will touch upon the role of insurance in retirement planning, including long-term care insurance, to protect against unforeseen circumstances.

Throughout this subchapter, we will include real-life examples, success stories, and expert advice to inspire readers on their journey towards financial success. By implementing the money management tips and retirement planning strategies discussed, individuals can gain confidence in their ability to achieve a prosperous and worry-free retirement.

Remember, retirement planning is not a one-time task, but an ongoing process. By being proactive and making smart money moves today, both teens and elders can build a solid financial foundation, ensuring a comfortable and financially secure retirement.

Insurance and Risk Management

Insurance is an essential component of financial planning and risk management. It provides protection against unforeseen events that could potentially have a significant financial impact on individuals and their families. In this subchapter, we will explore the importance of insurance and how it plays a crucial role in managing financial risks.

One of the key aspects of insurance is the concept of risk transfer. By paying a relatively small premium, individuals can transfer the financial risk associated with potential losses to an insurance company. This allows individuals to protect themselves from the potentially devastating financial consequences of events such as accidents, illnesses, natural disasters, and even death.

For teens, understanding the importance of insurance can be especially valuable as they start to navigate the world of personal finance. Whether it's obtaining car insurance before driving or considering health insurance options, having coverage in place can provide a safety net and peace of mind. By having insurance, teens can protect themselves and their families from unexpected medical expenses or liability claims.

Elders, on the other hand, have unique insurance needs that can change as they enter different stages of life. Retirement planning often involves considering long-term care insurance to cover potential medical expenses in the future. Additionally, life insurance can play a significant role in providing financial support for loved ones in the event of a passing, ensuring that debts are paid off and loved ones are taken care of.

When it comes to insurance, it's crucial to understand the different types available and determine the appropriate coverage for individual needs. This may include auto insurance, health insurance, homeowner's insurance, renter's insurance, or even umbrella insurance. Each type of insurance serves a specific purpose and offers varying levels of protection.

It's also important to review insurance policies periodically to ensure they adequately cover changing circumstances. As individuals enter different life stages, their insurance needs may evolve, requiring adjustments to coverage amounts or types of policies.

In conclusion, insurance and risk management are vital components of financial success for both teens and elders. By understanding the importance of insurance and obtaining appropriate coverage, individuals can protect themselves and their loved ones from unexpected financial burdens. Whether it's safeguarding against medical expenses, liability claims, or providing financial security for the future, insurance plays a crucial role in managing financial risks and ensuring peace of mind.

Estate Planning

Estate Planning: Securing Your Legacy for Generations to Come

Introduction:

Estate planning is a crucial aspect of financial success that often gets overlooked, especially by teens and elders. This subchapter aims to shed light on the importance of estate planning, providing valuable insights and practical tips for both age groups. Whether you're a young adult looking to secure your future or an elder interested in leaving a lasting legacy, this chapter will guide you through the process of estate planning.

Understanding Estate Planning:
Estate planning involves making crucial decisions about how your assets will be managed and distributed after your passing. It goes beyond just creating a will; it encompasses legal documents, financial arrangements, and medical directives. By engaging in estate planning, you ensure that your wishes are respected, minimize potential conflicts, and provide financial security for your loved ones.

Key Elements of Estate Planning:
. Writing a Will: A will is the cornerstone of estate planning. It allows you to specify how your assets should be distributed and who will be responsible for managing the process. We'll explore the importance of updating your will periodically and choosing an executor you trust.

Power of Attorney: This legal document grants a person of your choice the authority to make financial and legal decisions on your behalf in case you become incapacitated. We'll discuss the significance of choosing a reliable agent and the different types of power of attorney.

3. Healthcare Directives: Planning for medical emergencies is equally important. We'll delve into the significance of living wills, healthcare proxies, and do-not-resuscitate (DNR) orders, ensuring your preferences for medical treatments are respected.

4. Trusts: Trusts can be powerful tools to protect your assets and control their distribution. We'll explain the different types of trusts and their benefits, such as avoiding probate and minimizing estate taxes.

5. Charitable Giving: Estate planning provides a unique opportunity to leave a positive impact on society. We'll explore various ways you can include charitable giving in your estate plan, helping you support causes close to your heart.

Conclusion:

Estate planning is not just about ensuring the smooth transfer of assets; it's about securing your legacy and providing for future generations. By engaging in thoughtful estate planning, teens and elders can take control of their financial future, protect their loved ones, and leave a lasting impact on the world. So, take charge of you estate planning journey today and secure a prosperous future fo yourself and generations to come.

Setting Up an Emergency Fund

In today's uncertain world, it is crucial to have a financial safety net to protect yourself from unexpected events. Whether you are a teenager just starting your financial journey or an elder looking to secure your future, setting up an emergency fund should be a top priority. This subchapter will guide you through the process of establishing an emergency fund and explain its significance in managing your money effectively.

An emergency fund is a stash of money set aside specifically for unforeseen expenses or emergencies. These can range from medical emergencies, car repairs, or even sudden job loss. By having a robust emergency fund, you can avoid the stress and financial burden that often accompanies unexpected situations.

For teens, setting up an emergency fund can provide a sense of financial security. It allows you to become self-reliant and reduces the need to rely on your parents or guardians during emergencies. Start by setting a savings goal – aim to save at least three to six months' worth of expenses. This may seem daunting, but even small contributions add up over time. Consider opening a separate savings account dedicated solely to your emergency fund and automate regular transfers from your checking account to ensure consistent savings.

Elders can also benefit greatly from an emergency fund. As retirement approaches, unexpected expenses can disrupt your financial stability. Having an emergency fund will provide peace of mind and protect your hard-earned savings. Determine your monthly expenses and aim to save at least six to twelve months' worth. Explore low-risk investment options such as high-yield savings accounts or certificates of deposit (CDs) to grow your emergency fund while preserving your capital.

To maximize the growth of your emergency fund, consider implementing money management tips. Evaluate your spending habits and identify areas where you can cut back. Prioritize saving over unnecessary expenses and avoid accumulating debt. By practicing discipline and making conscious financial choices, you will be able to build a substantial emergency fund over time.

Remember, emergencies are a part of life, and being prepared is crucial. By setting up an emergency fund, you are taking a proactive step towards financial success. Whether you are a teen or an elder, the peace of mind that comes with having a safety net is invaluable. Start building your emergency fund today and enjoy the benefits of financial security.

Chapter 7: Entrepreneurship and Financial Independence

Exploring Entrepreneurial Opportunities

Introduction:

In today's fast-paced and ever-changing world, exploring entrepreneurial opportunities has become an exciting and viable option for individuals of all ages. Whether you are a teenager looking to earn some extra pocket money or an elder contemplating a second career, the world of entrepreneurship offers limitless possibilities. This subchapter aims to provide valuable insights and guidance on how to explore and seize entrepreneurial opportunities, ensuring financial success for teens and elders alike.

Identifying Your Passion and Skills:
The first step to exploring entrepreneurial opportunities is to identify your passion and skills. Take some time to reflect on what truly interests you and what you excel at. This could be anything from baking and crafting to digital marketing or financial management. By aligning your entrepreneurial venture with your passion and skills, you will not only enjoy what you do but also increase your chances of success.

Evaluating Market Demand:
Once you have identified your passion and skills, it is crucial to evaluate the market demand for your product or service. Conduct thorough research and analysis to understand your target audience, their needs, and competitors in the market. This will help you determine if there is a viable market for your entrepreneurial venture and allow you to make informed decisions.

Developing a Business Plan:
A well-structured business plan is essential for any entrepreneurial endeavor. It serves as a roadmap, outlining your goals, strategies, marketing plans, and financial projections. Take the time to carefully develop your business plan, seeking assistance from mentors or experts if necessary. This will not only help you stay focused but also attract potential investors or lenders.

Building a Support Network:
Building a support network is crucial for entrepreneurial success. Surround yourself with like-minded individuals, join business communities, attend networking events, and seek mentorship from experienced entrepreneurs. Learning from others' experiences, gaining insights, and receiving support will significantly enhance your entrepreneurial journey.

Securing Funding
Funding is often a vital aspect of starting and growing a business. As a teen or elder, there are various funding options available to you. Consider personal savings, crowdfunding, small business loans, grants or even seeking investors. Research and explore the funding option that best suit your needs and circumstances.

Conclusion:
Exploring entrepreneurial opportunities can be an incredibl rewarding and fulfilling experience, both financially and personally. B identifying your passion, evaluating market demand, developing business plan, building a support network, and securing funding, yo can embark on a successful entrepreneurial journey. Whether you a a teen looking to learn valuable skills or an elder seeking to start a ne chapter in life, entrepreneurship offers endless possibilities fc

financial success and personal growth. So, take the leap, seize the opportunity, and unlock your entrepreneurial potential.

Building a Business Plan

A well-crafted business plan is the foundation for any successful venture. Whether you are a young entrepreneur eager to start your own business or an experienced elder looking to turn your passion into a profitable venture, having a solid business plan is crucial. In this subchapter, we will explore the key elements of building a business plan and how it can pave the way to financial success.

1.   Executive   Summary:
The executive summary provides a concise overview of your business idea, including its objectives, target market, and competitive advantage. It should capture the attention of potential investors or lenders by highlighting the unique aspects of your venture.

2.   Market   Analysis.
Conduct a thorough market analysis to understand your target audience, industry trends, and competitors. This will enable you to identify opportunities and potential challenges, helping you make informed decisions and develop effective strategies.

3.   Company   Description
Describe your business in detail, including its legal structure, mission statement, and vision. Clearly articulate what sets your business apart from others and how it will meet the needs of your target market.

4.   Products   and   Service
Outline the specific products or services your business will offer and explain how they will benefit your customers. Emphasize the unique selling points that differentiate your offerings and provide competitive edge.

5.   Marketing   and   Sales   Strategy: Develop a comprehensive marketing and sales strategy to attract and retain customers. Identify your target market, outline your pricing strategy, and define the channels through which you will reach your audience. Consider leveraging digital platforms and social media to maximize your marketing efforts.

6.   Financial   Projections: Create realistic financial projections, including revenue forecasts, expenses, and profit margins. This will help you understand the financial viability of your business and demonstrate to potential investors or lenders that your venture is worth supporting.

7.   Operations   and   Management: Detail the operational aspects of your business, including staffing requirements, supply chain management, and production processes. Additionally, highlight the management team's qualifications and expertise, showcasing their ability to drive the success of your venture.

Remember, a business plan is not a static document. It should be regularly reviewed and updated as your business evolves. It will serve as a roadmap, helping you stay focused on your goals and navigate any challenges that arise.

By investing time and effort into building a comprehensive business plan, you will increase your chances of success and financial prosperity, whether you are a teen starting your first venture or an older pursuing a lifelong dream. Remember, with a solid business plan in hand, you are well-equipped to turn your entrepreneurial aspirations into reality.

Marketing and Sales Strategies

In today's fast-paced and highly competitive world, understanding effective marketing and sales strategies is crucial for individuals of all ages, including teens and elders. Whether you are a young person looking to launch your own business or an older individual seeking financial success, mastering these strategies will undoubtedly give you a competitive edge. This subchapter delves into the intricacies of marketing and sales, offering valuable insights and actionable tips to help you achieve your financial goals.

Firstly, it is important to recognize that marketing and sales go hand in hand. Marketing involves understanding your target audience, identifying their needs, and creating a compelling message that resonates with them. Sales, on the other hand, is the process of converting potential customers into actual buyers. By combining effective marketing techniques with strong sales skills, you can maximize your chances of success.

One key marketing strategy is to leverage the power of social media. Today's teens and elders are more connected than ever before, making platforms like Facebook, Instagram, and Twitter invaluable for reaching your target audience. By creating engaging content, utilizing relevant hashtags, and interacting with followers, you can build a loyal customer base and increase your brand awareness.

Another crucial aspect of marketing is developing a comprehensiv branding strategy. Your brand is a representation of your business an what it stands for. It encompasses your logo, website, packaging, an even your customer service. By consistently delivering a positive bran experience, you can establish trust and loyalty among your customers

When it comes to sales strategies, one of the most effective techniques is to focus on building relationships. People are more likely to buy from someone they trust and have a connection with. Take the time to understand your customers' needs and tailor your offerings accordingly. Additionally, providing exceptional customer service will not only result in repeat business but also generate positive word-of-mouth referrals.

Lastly, tracking and analyzing your marketing and sales efforts is essential for continuous improvement. Utilize tools such as Google Analytics to monitor website traffic, conversion rates, and customer behavior. By identifying what works and what doesn't, you can make data-driven decisions to optimize your strategies.

In conclusion, mastering marketing and sales strategies is paramount for financial success, regardless of age. By understanding your target audience, leveraging social media, developing a strong brand, building relationships, and analyzing your efforts, you can create a solid foundation for your business pursuits. So, whether you are a teen seeking to launch a successful startup or an elder looking to supplement your retirement income, these strategies will undoubtedly pave the way to financial prosperity.

Financial Independence and Wealth Creation

In today's fast-paced and ever-changing world, achieving financial independence and creating wealth has become a top priority for individuals of all ages. Whether you are a teenager just starting to earn money or an elder looking to secure your retirement, understanding the principles of money management and making smart money moves can lay the foundation for a financially successful future. This subchapter aims to provide essential insights and practical tips for both teens and elders to navigate the path towards financial independence and wealth creation.

For teens, developing good money management habits early on can have a significant impact on their financial well-being later in life. From setting realistic financial goals to budgeting and saving, this subchapter will guide teenagers on how to make their money work for them. It will emphasize the importance of saving a portion of their income, avoiding unnecessary debt, and making informed choices about spending and investing.

For elders, financial independence may take a different form, as they might be more focused on retirement planning and ensuring their financial security during their golden years. This subchapter will delve into strategies for saving for retirement, understanding different investment options, and making wise financial decisions to maximize their wealth. It will also shed light on the importance of estate planning, managing healthcare costs, and leaving a financial legacy for future generations.

Regardless of age, the principles of financial independence and wealth creation remain the same. This subchapter will explore various concepts such as compound interest, diversification, risk management and the power of long-term investing. It will provide real-life examples and success stories to inspire and motivate readers to take control of their financial futures.

Moreover, this subchapter will touch on the importance of financial education, recommending resources and tools that can help teens and elders gain a deeper understanding of personal finance. It will encourage readers to seek out mentors or financial advisors who can guide them on their journey towards financial independence.

By adopting the principles and strategies outlined in this subchapter, readers will be equipped with the knowledge and skills to make smart money moves, create wealth, and ultimately achieve financial independence. Whether you are a teen just starting your financial journey or an elder looking to secure your future, the path to financial success begins with taking control of your money and making informed decisions.

Remember, it's never too early or too late to start building a strong financial foundation. Start today and pave the way for a financially secure and prosperous future.

Chapter 8: Navigating Financial Challenges

Dealing with Financial Setbacks

Financial setbacks can happen to anyone, regardless of age or circumstances. Whether you are a teenager just starting your journey towards financial independence or an elder looking to manage your finances wisely, it is important to be prepared for unexpected challenges that may arise.

1. Create an Emergency Fund: One of the first steps towards dealing with financial setbacks is to establish an emergency fund. This fund should ideally cover three to six months' worth of living expenses. By setting aside a portion of your income regularly, you can ensure that you have a safety net to fall back on in times of crisis.

2. Evaluate Your Spending Habits: Take a close look at your spending habits and identify areas where you can cut back. This may involve reducing discretionary expenses such as eating out or entertainment. By making small adjustments to your lifestyle, you can free up more funds to deal with financial setbacks.

3. Seek Professional Advice: If you find yourself overwhelmed by financial setbacks, don't hesitate to seek professional advice. Financial advisors can provide valuable guidance and help you create a tailored plan to overcome your specific challenges. They can also offer insight into investment strategies and retirement planning, ensuring long-term financial security.

4. Prioritize Debt Repayment: If you have outstanding debts, it crucial to prioritize their repayment. Start by paying off high-interest debts first, as they tend to accumulate quickly and can become

significant burden. Consider consolidating your debts or negotiating with creditors to establish more favorable repayment terms.

5. Stay Positive and Stay Focused: Dealing with financial setbacks can be emotionally draining. It is essential to stay positive and maintain a clear focus on your long-term financial goals. Remember that setbacks are temporary, and with determination and perseverance, you can overcome them.

6. Educate Yourself: Take advantage of the numerous resources available to learn more about money management. Books, articles, and online courses can provide valuable insights into budgeting, investing, and other financial topics. By continuously educating yourself, you can make informed decisions and avoid future setbacks.

In conclusion, financial setbacks are a part of life, but they don't have to define your financial future. By following these tips and developing good money management habits, both teens and elders can navigate through financial challenges and achieve long-term financial success. Remember, it's never too early or too late to take control of your finances and secure a brighter financial future.

Overcoming Financial Obstacles

Financial obstacles can arise at any point in our lives, and it is crucial to develop the skills and mindset necessary to overcome them. This subchapter aims to provide valuable insights and strategies for both teens and elders to navigate and conquer various financial challenges.

For teens, one of the most common obstacles they face is managing their money effectively. It is essential to develop good financial habits early on to set a solid foundation for a successful financial future. One important tip is to create a budget and stick to it. By tracking income and expenses, teens can gain a better understanding of their financial situation and make informed decisions. Additionally, it is crucial to prioritize needs over wants and avoid unnecessary spending. Saving money regularly, even if it is in small amounts, can go a long way in building a financial safety net and preparing for future goals.

Elders, on the other hand, may face different financial obstacles, such as planning for retirement or managing limited income. Retirement planning is crucial to ensure a comfortable and stress-free future. It is important to explore different retirement savings options, such as individual retirement accounts (IRAs) or employer-sponsored plans and contribute regularly. Seeking professional advice from financial advisors or retirement planners can also provide guidance tailored to your specific needs and goals.

Furthermore, managing limited income can be challenging for elders. Cutting unnecessary expenses and finding ways to save money can make a significant difference. Exploring cost-saving options, such as downsizing living arrangements or taking advantage of senior discounts, can help stretch limited funds. Additionally, considering part-time employment or exploring freelance opportunities can provide additional income streams.

Regardless of age, it is important to be proactive and resourceful when facing financial obstacles. Developing a mindset of resilience and adaptability is key to overcoming challenges. Seeking financial education and staying informed about personal finance topics can empower individuals to make smart money moves. Moreover, building a support network of like-minded individuals or joining financial communities can provide valuable insights and support during difficult times.

By adopting these strategies and embracing a proactive attitude, both teens and elders can overcome financial obstacles and achieve long-term financial success. Remember, it is never too early or too late to take control of your finances and secure a brighter financial future.

Strategies for Recovering from Debt

Introduction:

Debt can be a heavy burden and can cause stress and anxiety, affecting not only our finances but also our overall well-being. Whether you are a teenager just starting to manage your money or an elder looking to improve your financial situation, it's never too late to take control of your debt and work towards financial freedom. In this subchapter, we will explore effective strategies for recovering from debt and regaining control over your finances.

1. Assess Your Situation:

The first step towards recovering from debt is to assess your current financial situation. Take a close look at your income, expenses, and debts. List all outstanding debts, including their interest rates and minimum monthly payments. This will help you prioritize which debts to tackle first.

2. Create a Budget:

Developing a realistic budget is crucial for managing your money effectively. Track your expenses and identify areas where you can cut back. Allocate a portion of your income towards debt repayment, ensuring you pay more than the minimum due whenever possible. Stick to your budget religiously to avoid accumulating additional debt.

3. Prioritize and Negotiate:

Evaluate your debts and prioritize them based on interest rates and outstanding balances. Consider negotiating with creditors to lower interest rates or establish a more affordable repayment plan. Man creditors are willing to work with individuals who demonstrate commitment towards repaying their debts.

4. Debt Consolidation:

If you have multiple debts with high-interest rates, consider consolidating them into a single loan with a lower interest rate. Debt consolidation simplifies your payments and can potentially save you money in interest over time.

5. Increase Your Income:

Boosting your income can accelerate your debt recovery process. Look for opportunities to earn extra money, such as part-time jobs, freelance work, or selling unused items. Redirect this additional income towards paying off your debts.

6. Seek Professional Help:

If you find it challenging to handle your debts alone, don't hesitate to seek professional assistance. Credit counseling agencies or financial advisors can provide guidance and support to help you develop a personalized debt repayment plan.

Conclusion:

Recovering from debt requires commitment, discipline, and patience. By following these strategies, you can take control of your financial situation and work towards a debt-free future. Remember, it's never too late to start managing your money wisely, whether you're a teenager or an elder. Empower yourself with financial knowledge, implement these strategies, and pave the way to financial success.

Seeking Professional Financial Assistance

In today's complex financial landscape, seeking professional financial assistance is a smart step towards securing your financial future. Whether you are a teenager taking your first steps towards financial independence or an elder looking to maximize your retirement savings, professional guidance can make a significant difference in your financial success.

One of the primary reasons to seek professional financial assistance is to gain expert advice tailored to your specific needs. Financial professionals possess a deep understanding of the intricacies of money management, investment strategies, and retirement planning. By working with a professional, you can benefit from their years of experience and knowledge, enabling you to make informed decisions and avoid costly mistakes.

For teenagers, professional financial assistance can provide valuable guidance during a crucial period of learning and growth. Money management tips for teens can range from opening a savings account to understanding the basics of budgeting and investing. A financial advisor can help you develop a solid foundation for financial success teaching you how to set financial goals, create a budget, and make informed decisions about saving and spending.

For elders, professional assistance is equally essential, especially when it comes to retirement planning. As you near retirement, it becomes crucial to assess your financial situation, estimate your retirement needs, and develop a comprehensive plan. A financial advisor can help you navigate the complexities of retirement accounts, social security benefits, and investment strategies to maximize your savings and ensure a comfortable retirement.

Furthermore, seeking professional financial assistance provides peace of mind. Money matters can be overwhelming and stressful, but working with a financial professional can alleviate much of the anxiety associated with financial decision-making. They can help you identify potential risks, manage your investments, and adjust your financial plan as needed, allowing you to focus on other aspects of your life.

When selecting a financial professional, it is crucial to choose someone who is reputable, qualified, and has a fiduciary duty to act in your best interest. Look for advisors who hold relevant certifications, such as Certified Financial Planner (CFP), and have a track record of success in managing finances for individuals in your age group.

In conclusion, seeking professional financial assistance is an essential step towards financial success, whether you are a teenager or an elder. By leveraging the expertise of financial professionals, you can gain valuable insights, make informed decisions, and secure your financial future. Remember, it is never too early or too late to seek professional help for managing your money effectively.

Chapter 9: Money and Relationships

Managing Joint Finances

Money management is a crucial skill that everyone should learn, regardless of their age. Whether you are a teenager just starting to earn your own money or an elder looking to make the most of your retirement savings, understanding how to manage joint finances is essential. In this subchapter, we will explore some practical tips and strategies to help you effectively manage your money as a team.

One of the first steps in managing joint finances is open and honest communication. Sit down with your partner, spouse, or family members and discuss your financial goals, expectations, and concerns. This will help you establish a common understanding and create a solid foundation for making financial decisions together. It is important to remember that managing joint finances is a team effort, and everyone's input should be valued.

Creating a budget is another essential tool for managing joint finances Start by tracking your income and expenses to get a clear picture of where your money goes each month. Identify areas where you can cut back on unnecessary expenses and allocate funds towards your financial goals, such as saving for a down payment on a house or planning for retirement. Remember to revisit and adjust your budget regularly to accommodate any changes in your financial situation.

Transparency is key when managing joint finances. Keep each other informed about your individual spending and savings habits. Regularly review bank statements, credit card bills, and other financial documents together to ensure that you are both on the same page. This will help prevent any surprises or misunderstandings down the road.

Consider setting joint financial goals as a way to stay motivated and focused. Work together to establish short-term and long-term objectives, such as paying off debt, saving for a dream vacation, or building an emergency fund. Celebrate milestones along the way to keep the momentum going and strengthen your financial partnership.

Lastly, seek professional advice when needed. Financial advisors or counselors can provide guidance and expertise tailored to your specific financial situation. They can help you develop strategies for managing joint finances, create investment plans, and ensure that you are making informed decisions.

In conclusion, managing joint finances requires open communication, budgeting, transparency, goal-setting, and professional advice when necessary. By implementing these strategies, you can work together as a team towards financial success, whether you are a teenager just starting to learn about money management or an elder looking to make the most of your retirement savings. Remember, it's never too early or too late to start managing your joint finances effectively.

Communicating about Money

Effective communication about money is essential for both teens and elders to achieve financial success. In this subchapter, we will explore the importance of open and honest discussions surrounding personal finances, as well as provide practical tips for effective communication about money management.

For teens, discussing money matters with their parents or guardians is crucial in developing a strong foundation for financial literacy. Parents should create an open and non-judgmental environment where teens feel comfortable asking questions and seeking guidance. By initiating conversations about budgeting, saving, and investing, parents can empower their teens to make informed financial decisions.

Similarly, elders can benefit from discussing money matters with their loved ones or financial advisors. With retirement planning, healthcare expenses, and estate management becoming increasingly complex, elders must engage in open communication to ensure their financial well-being. Sharing their financial goals and concerns with family members or professionals can provide valuable insights and support.

Here are some practical tips for effective communication about money:

1. Active Listening: When engaging in money-related discussions, it is crucial to listen attentively and empathetically. This will help foster understanding and encourage open dialogue.

2. Setting Shared Goals: Whether it's saving for a vacation or planning for retirement, setting shared financial goals can create a sense of teamwork and motivation. Regularly revisiting these goals will help track progress and make necessary adjustments.

3. Transparency: Honesty is key when discussing financial matters. Share information about income, debts, and expenses to gain a comprehensive understanding of the overall financial situation.

4. Avoiding Judgment: It is important to maintain a non-judgmental attitude during money conversations. By creating a safe space, teens and elders will feel more comfortable sharing their financial challenges and seeking guidance.

5. Seeking Professional Advice: Encourage both teens and elders to seek guidance from financial advisors or experts. These professionals can provide personalized advice based on individual circumstances and help make informed financial decisions.

By fostering effective communication about money, teens can gain valuable financial skills and elders can secure their financial future. Open discussions, active listening, and seeking professional advice are the building blocks for successful money management. Whether you're a teen learning to navigate the world of personal finance or an elder planning for retirement, communicating about money is an essential skill for financial success.

Preparing for Financial Milestones

In life, we all experience various financial milestones that require careful planning and preparation. Whether you are a teenager just starting to explore the world of money or an elder looking to ensure a secure financial future, it is essential to have a solid foundation of money management skills. This subchapter will provide valuable tips and strategies to help you navigate these milestones successfully.

For   Teens:

1. Set Financial Goals: Start by defining your short-term and long-term financial goals. This could include saving for college, buying your first car, or even starting a business. Having clear goals will help you stay focused and motivated.

2. Create a Budget: Develop a budget to track your income and expenses. This will help you understand where your money is going and make adjustments as needed. Remember to save a portion of your income regularly and prioritize your spending.

3. Learn to Save: Cultivate the habit of saving early on. Start by setting aside a portion of your allowance or part-time job earnings into savings account. Consider opening a high-yield savings account to maximize your savings potential.

4. Understand Credit: Educate yourself on the concept of credit and the importance of maintaining a good credit score. Use credit responsibly and make payments on time to build a positive credit history.

For   Elder

1. Retirement Planning: Start planning for retirement as early possible. Calculate your desired retirement income and explore

various retirement savings options such as 401(k) plans, IRAs, and pensions. Consider seeking professional advice to ensure you are on track to meet your retirement goals.

2. Estate Planning: Make sure you have a will in place to outline how your assets will be distributed after your passing. Consider consulting an estate planning attorney to navigate the complexities of estate taxes and ensure your wishes are carried out.

3. Review Insurance Coverage: Regularly review your insurance policies, including health, life, and long-term care insurance. Ensure you have adequate coverage to protect yourself and your loved ones from unforeseen events.

4. Social Security Benefits: Familiarize yourself with the Social Security system and understand when and how to claim your benefits. Consider factors such as your health, life expectancy, and financial needs before making this decision.

By preparing for financial milestones, you can set yourself up for a successful and secure future. Whether you are a teen or an elder, implementing these money management tips will help you achieve financial success and peace of mind. Remember, it's never too early or too late to start taking control of your finances.

Strategies for Financially Healthy Relationships

In today's world, maintaining healthy relationships is not just about emotional compatibility but also about financial harmony. Money matters can often become a significant source of stress and conflict in relationships, whether between teenagers or elderly couples. Therefore, it is crucial to develop effective strategies for achieving financial success together. This subchapter aims to provide valuable insights and practical tips on managing money and fostering financially healthy relationships, catering to both the general audience and the specific niches of teenagers and elders.

One of the fundamental strategies for achieving financial harmony is open and honest communication about money. It is essential to establish a safe space where both partners can openly discuss their financial goals, aspirations, and concerns. Regularly discussing income, expenses, and financial decisions can help avoid misunderstandings and build trust.

Another key strategy is creating a budget together. This applies to all age groups, as budgeting is a vital skill for managing personal finances. By setting financial goals and allocating resources effectively, couples can control spending, save for the future, and avoid unnecessary debt. Involving teenagers in budgeting discussions can help them develop responsible financial habits early on, while elders can benefit from revisiting their budget as their circumstances change.

Furthermore, it is important to establish shared financial goals. Whether it's saving for a family vacation, buying a house, or planning for retirement, working towards common objectives can strengthen the bond between partners. Encouraging teenagers to set financial goals, such as saving for college or a car, can also instill a sense of purpose and discipline.

In addition to setting goals, it is crucial to prioritize financial independence. Encouraging teenagers to earn their own money through part-time jobs or entrepreneurial ventures teaches them the value of hard work and financial self-reliance. For elders, maintaining financial independence may involve creating a retirement plan that ensures a comfortable and worry-free future.

Lastly, understanding each other's financial values and attitudes is vital. Some individuals are natural savers, while others may be more inclined to spend. Recognizing and respecting these differences can help avoid conflicts and facilitate compromise. It is important to find a balance that respects personal financial styles while working towards shared goals.

By implementing these strategies, individuals can cultivate financially healthy relationships, regardless of their age. Whether you are a teenager learning to manage your money or an elder navigating retirement, these tips will empower you to make smart money moves, fostering financial success and harmony in your relationships.

Chapter 10: Building a Lifetime of Financial Success

Reviewing and Revising Financial Goals

In the journey towards financial success, it is crucial to regularly review and revise your financial goals. This subchapter will guide you through the importance of reviewing your goals and provide tips on how to effectively revise them.

Financial goals act as guiding stars, helping us make wise financial decisions and stay on track. However, life is dynamic, and our circumstances change over time. Therefore, it is essential to periodically review our financial goals to ensure they align with our current needs and aspirations.

For teens, reviewing financial goals is particularly important as they transition into adulthood and face new financial responsibilities. As you gain more independence and start earning money, it is crucial to reassess your goals to accommodate new priorities and aspirations. Are you saving for higher education? Are you planning to buy a car? Reviewing your goals will help you determine if they are still realistic and adjust them accordingly.

Elders, too, can benefit from reviewing and revising their financial goals. Retirement brings a significant shift in financial needs and priorities. By periodically reviewing your goals, you can ensure that your retirement savings are on track and adjust your plans to accommodate any unforeseen circumstances.

Here are some tips to effectively review and revise your financial goals:

1. Evaluate your current financial situation: Take stock of your income, expenses, debts, and savings. This will help you understand

your financial standing and identify any gaps or areas that need improvement.

2. Assess your goals: Are your goals still relevant? Do they align with your current financial situation and aspirations? Evaluate whether you need to adjust your goals or set new ones.

3. Break down your goals: Divide your goals into short-term, medium-term, and long-term objectives. This will make them more manageable and allow you to track your progress more effectively.

4. Seek professional advice: Consider consulting with a financial advisor who can provide expert guidance and help you make informed decisions about your goals and financial plans.

5. Stay flexible: Remember that life is unpredictable, and circumstances may change. Be open to adjusting your goals as needed and regularly review your progress to ensure you are on the right path.

By regularly reviewing and revising your financial goals, you can adapt to life's changes and increase your chances of achieving financial success. Whether you are a teen or an elder, taking the time to assess your goals will empower you to make smart money moves and secure prosperous future.

Continuing Education in Personal Finance

In today's ever-changing financial landscape, it is crucial for individuals of all ages to continually educate themselves on personal finance. Whether you are a teenager just starting to navigate the world of money or an elder looking to secure your financial future, the importance of staying informed and knowledgeable cannot be overstated. This subchapter aims to provide valuable insights and money management tips for both teens and elders, helping them make smart money moves and achieve financial success.

For teens, understanding the basics of personal finance is essential as they begin to take on more financial responsibilities. From managing an allowance to budgeting for college expenses, learning early on how to handle money can set the foundation for a lifetime of financial wellness. This subchapter will delve into the key aspects of financial literacy for teens, introducing concepts such as budgeting, saving, investing, and debt management. It will also provide practical tips on how to develop good financial habits, make informed spending decisions, and avoid common financial pitfalls.

For elders, continuing education in personal finance becomes equally important as they plan for retirement and manage their savings. This subchapter will address the specific financial concerns faced by elders, such as retirement planning, healthcare costs, estate planning, and protecting assets. It will offer guidance on how to make the most out of retirement accounts, navigate social security benefits, and create sustainable income stream during retirement. Additionally, it will discuss strategies for preserving wealth and passing it on to future generations.

Regardless of age, the rapidly evolving financial landscape requires individuals to stay up to date with the latest trends and tools in personal finance. This subchapter will emphasize the importance of ongoing education and provide resources for individuals to continue learning about money management. It will explore various mediums, including books, podcasts, online courses, and workshops, that can help individuals expand their financial knowledge and refine their money management skills.

By investing in their financial education, both teens and elders can make informed decisions, grow their wealth, and achieve financial success. This subchapter aims to empower readers with the knowledge and tools necessary to navigate the complex world of personal finance, ensuring a secure and prosperous future for themselves and their families.

Remember, it is never too early or too late to start learning about personal finance. Let this subchapter be your guide as you embark on a journey towards financial success.

Teaching Financial Literacy to Others

Financial literacy is a crucial life skill that everyone should possess, regardless of age. In this subchapter, we will explore the importance of teaching financial literacy to others, with a particular focus on teenagers and elders. By imparting knowledge and offering practical money management tips, we can empower individuals from both generations to make informed financial decisions and achieve financial success.

Teens often face the daunting task of managing their finances for the first time. As they transition into adulthood, it becomes essential to equip them with the necessary tools and knowledge to navigate the complex world of money. By teaching financial literacy to teenagers, we can help them develop healthy financial habits that will benefit them throughout their lives. From budgeting and saving to understanding credit and debt, these foundational skills can set them on the path to financial independence and security.

Elders, on the other hand, may have already accumulated a wealth of financial experience but could benefit from an update on the ever-changing financial landscape. As retirement approaches, it becomes crucial for elders to have a solid understanding of investment options, social security benefits, and estate planning. By teaching financial literacy to elders, we can help ensure a smooth transition into retirement and empower them to make informed decisions about their financial future.

When teaching financial literacy to others, it is essential to use variety of teaching methods and resources. Visual aids, real-life examples, and interactive exercises can make the learning process engaging and effective. Additionally, tailoring the content to the specific needs and interests of the audience is crucial. For example, discussing the importance of saving for college may resonate more with teenagers, while explaining retirement planning may be more relevant to elders.

Furthermore, it is essential to emphasize the practical application of financial literacy skills. Encourage teenagers to create budgets, open bank accounts, and start saving early. For elders, provide guidance on investment strategies and estate planning options. By incorporating hands-on activities and practical advice, individuals can see the immediate benefits of financial literacy in their lives.

In conclusion, teaching financial literacy to others is a powerful way to empower individuals to make sound financial decisions. By targeting teenagers and elders with tailored money management tips, we can equip them with the skills necessary for financial success. Whether it is building a strong financial foundation for teens or helping elders navigate retirement, financial literacy is an invaluable tool that benefits individuals of all ages.

Celebrating Financial Milestones

In our journey towards financial success, it is crucial to acknowledge and celebrate the milestones we achieve along the way. These milestones not only serve as markers of our progress but also motivate and inspire us to continue making smart money moves. Whether you are a teenager just starting to navigate the world of finance or an elder looking to enhance your money management skills, celebrating your financial milestones is essential for long-term success.

For teens, financial milestones can be as simple as saving a certain amount of money or successfully budgeting for a desired item. It is important to recognize and reward yourself for these achievements, as they lay the foundation for responsible money management habits in the future. By celebrating these milestones, you reinforce positive financial behaviors and foster a sense of accomplishment, encouraging you to make smart money moves in the years to come.

As elders, financial milestones can take on a different significance. Perhaps you have successfully paid off a large debt or reached a saving goal that seemed unattainable. These achievements are worth celebrating and can provide a sense of security and peace of mind. By acknowledging these milestones, you not only recognize your own efforts but also set an example for others, illustrating that it is never too late to take control of your finances and achieve financial success.

Celebrating financial milestones can take various forms. It could involve treating yourself to a small indulgence or planning a special outing with loved ones. However, it is important to strike a balance between celebration and staying on track with your financial goals. You can set aside a specific budget for celebrations, ensuring that they do not derail your progress.

Moreover, celebrating financial milestones is not just about individual achievements but also about fostering a supportive community. By sharing your milestones with others, you can inspire and motivate those around you to take control of their finances. This can be particularly impactful for teens, as they learn from the experiences and successes of their elders.

In conclusion, celebrating financial milestones is a vital aspect of the journey towards financial success. Whether you are a teenager or an elder, recognizing and rewarding your achievements helps reinforce positive money management habits and provides a sense of accomplishment. By striking a balance between celebration and staying on track with your goals, you can create a supportive community that inspires others to make smart money moves. So, let's raise a toast to our financial milestones and keep moving forward on the path to financial success!

Milton Keynes UK
Ingram Content Group UK Ltd.
UKHW020930231123
433129UK00016B/852